W9-ART-436

· I Want to Know™ ·

About THE TEN COMMANDMENTS

Rick Osborne and K. Christie Bowler

Zonderkidz

The Children's Group of ZondervanPublishingHouse

For Lightwave
Managing Editor:
  Elaine Osborne
Art Director:
  Terry Van Roon

Ten Commandments copyright © 1998 by The Zondervan Corporation.

Artwork and Text copyright © 1998 by Lightwave Publishing Inc. All rights reserved. http://www.lightwavepublishing.com

Scripture portions taken from the *Holy Bible, New International Reader's Version* Copyright © 1994, 1996 by International Bible Society.

All rights reserved. No part of this publication may be reproduced, stored in a retrieval system, or transmitted in any form or by any means—electronic, mechanical, photocopy, recording, or any other— except for brief quotations in printed reviews, without the prior permission of the publisher.

The photos used on pages 7, 15, and 25 were obtained from Corel Corporation's Professional Photo CD collection.
The images used on page 9, 11, 14, 16, 17, 22, and 25 were obtained from ISMI's Master Photos Collection, 1895 Francisco Blvd. East, San Rafael, CA 94901-5506.
Photos on page 18 and 32 © 1998 Ron Nickle.
Photo on page 20 © 1998 F22 Photography.

Library of Congress Cataloging-in-Publication Data

Osborne, Rick, 1961–   .
      The Ten commandments : what they are and why they're still important for me today / Rick Osborne and K. Christie Bowler.
            p.   cm.—(I want to know™)
      Summary: Identifies the Ten Commandments, tells the story behind them, places them in a Christian context, and discusses why they are important and how they can be applied today.
      ISBN 0–310–22095–5 (hardcover)
      1. Ten commandments—Juvenile literature.
2. Christian ethics—Juvenile literature.   [1. Ten commandments. 2. Christian life.] I. Bowler, K. Christie, 1958–   . II. Title. III. Series: Osborne, Rick, 1961–   . I want to know™.
BV4656.073   1999
241.5'2—dc21   98-11683
                                                 CIP
                                                 AC

This edition is printed on acid-free paper and meets the American National Standards Institute Z39.48 standard.

Published by Zondervan Publishing House, Grand Rapids, Michigan 49530, U.S.A. http://www.zondervan.com

Printed in China.

All rights reserved.

Building Christian faith in families

A Lightwave Production
P.O. Box 160 Maple Ridge
B.C., Canada V2X 7G1

99 00 /HK/ 5 4 3 2

Contents

The Story of the Ten Commandments 4–5
Laws from a Mountain, The Mess, The Logic of the Laws

Laws of Other Cultures 6–7
Worldwide Rules, Hammurabi or God?, The Ten Commandments Are Unique

Commandment One: **No Other Gods** 8–9
God's ABC, Adam and Eve's Choice, The List

Commandment Two: **Don't Make or Worship Idols** 10–11
God or Idol?, Idol Temptations, Idols Today

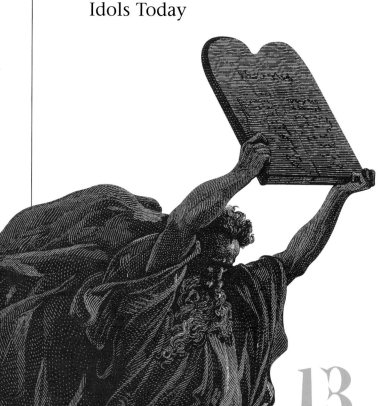

Commandment Eight: **Don't Steal**................22–23
To Lock or Not?, Greed or Generosity?, More Than Possessions

Commandment Nine: **Don't Lie**................................24–25
Little Is Big, Spaghetti Castle?, Build 'Em Up, Positive Communication

Commandment Ten: **Don't Covet**................................26–27
Start Right, Never Just One, The Thought Counts, Garbage In, Garbage Out

The Heart of It................28–29
By Heart, Carved by Love, Growing the Relationship

Is It Wrong?............................30–31

Strong Foundation..................32
Build Wisely, Bedrock Love

Commandment Three: **Don't Misuse God's Name**....................12–13
What's in a Name?, Truth Only, Swearing

Commandment Four: **Keep the Sabbath**..........................14–15
Jesus: The Sabbath, Twice Reminded, From Saturday to Sunday

Commandment Five: **Honor Your Parents**..........................16–17
Listen to Mom, What Skills!, My Way, Honor "How-To's"

Commandment Six: **Don't Murder**..............................18–19
Laser Mind, Life Is a Gift, The Two Greatest Commandments

Commandment Seven: **Don't Commit Adultery**..........................20–21
First People First, Number-One Promise, Broken Hearts, Hollywood

32

The Story of the Ten Commandments

Laws from a Mountain

Imagine if there were no rules and you could do whatever you wanted. Awesome freedom? No. Awful mess! Why? Because God gave us rules and laws to protect us and help us have great lives—not to make life hard. His laws show us how he made life to work best. God's most famous laws are the Ten Commandments, which he first gave to Moses and the Israelites.

The Israelites were slaves in Egypt. Pharaoh, Egypt's king, made life difficult for them until they cried out to God. God used a burning bush to get Moses to help them. Then, with ten awesome plagues, God convinced Pharaoh to let the Israelites go. Moses took them to Mount Sinai where God put on a spectacular display of power with lightning, fire, and an earthquake. Then he spoke to them from the mountain. He said he'd rescued them so they could be his people. Their part was to obey his commands. Moses went up the mountain to meet with God, and God wrote the Ten Commandments on two stone tablets.

The Mess

Why do we need God's commandments? When God made the first people, Adam and Eve, there was only one law: Don't eat from the tree of the knowledge of good and evil.

The Fall—long, long ago.

To get ready for the flood, Noah builds a big boat.

God tells Abraham to go to Canaan and promises him a son.

3940 B.C. or 10,000 B.C.

2285 B.C. or 8285 B.C.

God's laws were in Adam and Eve's hearts. They knew what was right. At first, nothing separated them from God. Then Satan, God's enemy, lied to them, saying the tree's fruit could make them be like God. They believed Satan and ate from the tree. BIG MISTAKE!

Adam and Eve's disobedience broke God's law. That sin separated them from God. Everyone born after them was born sinful and separated from God, too. The results showed up quickly: Adam and Eve's son killed his own brother! Instead of knowing and doing what was right, people did whatever they wanted. But it wasn't fun at all! They were selfish, greedy, proud, and mean. God was very sad, but he had a plan to fix everything. First, he destroyed the wickedness on the earth with a flood so people would know that sin led to punishment.

Only Noah's family survived. Through his descendants, Abraham and Sarah, God built the Israelite nation and gave them his laws so people would again know what was right and wrong. This was the first step in God's plan to wipe out sin and make our hearts right with him again.

The Logic of the Laws

The Ten Commandments are in a special order. God starts with the most important commandments. One to Three tell us to love and honor God in our hearts and with our actions and words. Obeying them makes obeying the others possible. Number Four links the first three, about loving God, to the last six, about loving people. Five shows us God's plan for how we learn to obey God and love people. Six tells us to love people from our hearts and respect life. Seven tells us how to keep our most important relationships safe. Eight and Nine tell us to love people with our actions and words. And Ten tells us to keep our inner thoughts and attitudes right, which is the key to obeying all the rest.

Jacob and his family move to Egypt.

The Exodus—when God leads the Israelites out of Egypt.

God gives Moses the Ten Commandments.

1920 B.C.   1705 B.C. (possibly)   1275 B.C.

Laws of Other Cultures

Worldwide Rules

So who needs the commands God gave Moses? Everyone!

If you play basketball or volleyball in North America, can you play in Europe, Asia, or Africa? Of course! But imagine trying to play basketball if everywhere you went the courts, balls, and rules were different! Thankfully, the basic rules are a core part of the game wherever it's played. That's because all games of basketball come from the same first game with the same first rules.

The rules for people are like that, too. The same laws are good for all people in all times and all places. Why? Because God's rules come out of who God is and how he made life to work—and that doesn't change.

This is Hammurabi's black stele with his laws carved on it.

God's laws were around long before Moses. Everyone knows basic right and wrong. Almost every civilization that we know about has had rules against things like stealing, lying, murder, adultery, and disrespect of parents. Where would so many different nations get the same ideas of right and wrong unless there really was only one right way—God's way? These laws came from the same first "rules." They came from the same God who designed life and people to work in a certain way.

Hammurabi or God?

Throughout history, God has shared his laws with people, showing them who he is and what he's like. For example, look at Hammurabi who was the king of Babylon around three hundred years before Moses. He had his laws carved into a black rock or *stele*, which we still have today. Hammurabi's laws dealt with some of the same things as the laws God would later give to Moses—including stealing, adultery, and lying.

God's laws never change. They're always right and they apply to all people, everywhere, all the time. It's *always* wrong to do things like lie, steal, and murder. That never changes because God never does

Some Jewish men wear phylacteries to remind them about God's law. These are boxes strapped on their arms that contain Bible verses about keeping God's laws.

those things. And if people do them, look out! They end up with broken relationships and no trust—youch! But when we obey God's laws, our relationships grow deep and strong, people trust us, we get good reputations, and people want to be around us—all right!

God's laws are always the same. Finding the same laws in so many nations and so many centuries proves this is true.

The Ten Commandments Are Unique

Beginning when Adam and Eve were sent out of the Garden, people's relationships with God went downhill—until they even forgot who God was! With this relationship wrecked, people served made-up gods instead of the true God. In fact, the people who lived in Hammurabi's Babylon served a lot of "gods."

But God wanted people to know about him again and have a relationship with him, so in the Ten Commandments he gave laws that let his people know who he was and how they should act toward him. No nation but Israel had these laws about *monotheism* (the belief that there is only one God). A relationship with the one God, and living in line with how he made things to work, is the only way to have a great life. No other nation's laws included monotheism because Israel was the only nation that had a relationship with God.

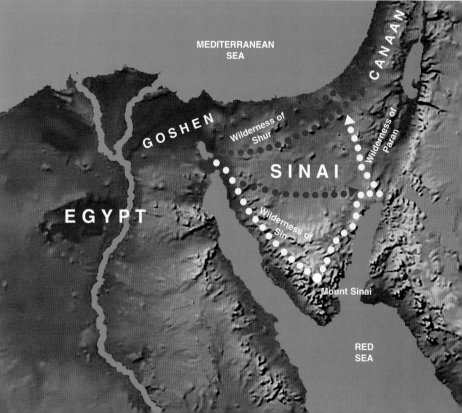

LEGEND
○ ○ ○ Possible routes of the Exodus
● ● ● Traditional route of the Exodus

MEDITERRANEAN SEA

GOSHEN

Wilderness of Shur

CANAAN

SINAI

Wilderness of Paran

EGYPT

Wilderness of Sin

Mount Sinai

RED SEA

Commandment One:
No Other Gods

God's ABC

Now that we know why we need laws and where the Ten Commandments came from, let's take a closer look at each commandment.

What's the first thing you're taught when you set out to learn something? In tennis and baseball you learn how to hold the racquet or bat. In music you learn the notes. In school we start with ABC and 1–2–3. We start with the lesson that everything else depends on. When we get that right, the other things fall into place. But if we don't, we always have trouble with the rest.

In the same way, the first commandment God gave to Moses was the foundation for all the others: *"Do not put any other gods in place of me"* (Exodus 20:3). Before anything else, we need the right relationship with

God *in our hearts*. This is for our good. If we put anything else in God's place, we're not trusting God as our Father or letting him love, guide, teach, and protect us.

Adam and Eve's Choice

Adam and Eve's first sin broke this commandment. They listened to Satan's lie and believed that they could figure things out for themselves and choose a better way than God's. Adam and Eve stopped trusting God's love and care for them. When they didn't trust God, what they did trust became their god.

Adam and Eve didn't understand that God *is* love! He's unselfish. Everything he does and says comes out of his love for us. This relationship with God is the core of all God's laws. God gives us laws so that we'll have great lives. They're for our good. God tells us to put him first because he knows that putting him first is the very best thing for us. When we focus on God, all the other things flow out of that. There is no better way. God knows everything, so as we trust him and do things his way, our lives work out for the best.

Just as learning our ABCs allows us to read, putting our trust in God gives us great lives. What a payoff!

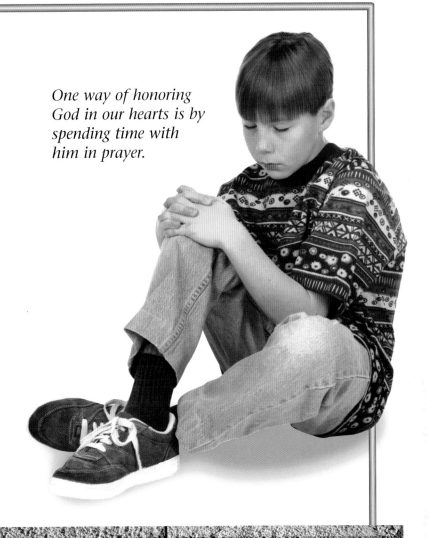

One way of honoring God in our hearts is by spending time with him in prayer.

The List

The Ten Commandments weren't numbered when they were first written down in the Bible. So, over the centuries, different groups of people numbered the commandments differently. But the effect is the same. Here are three main ways they were numbered:

1

1. I am the Lord your God.
2. Don't have other gods or make or worship idols.
3. Don't misuse God's name.
4. Keep the Sabbath holy.
5. Honor your parents.
6. Don't murder.
7. Don't commit adultery.
8. Don't steal.
9. Don't give false witness.
10. Don't covet.

2

1. Don't have other gods.
2. Don't misuse God's name.
3. Keep the Sabbath holy.
4. Honor your parents.
5. Don't murder.
6. Don't commit adultery.
7. Don't steal.
8. Don't give false witness.
9. Don't covet your neighbor's wife.
10. Don't covet your neighbor's things.

3

1. Don't have other gods.
2. Don't make or worship idols.
3. Don't misuse God's name.
4. Keep the Sabbath holy.
5. Honor your parents.
6. Don't murder.
7. Don't commit adultery.
8. Don't steal.
9. Don't give false witness.
10. Don't covet.

In this book we're using the third list.

Commandment Two:
Don't Make or Worship Idols

God or Idol?

We can tell what's most important to people by how they act. That's what the second commandment is about: *"Do not make statues of gods. . . . Do not bow down to them or worship them"* (Exodus 20:4–5). If God is first in our hearts, he'll also be first *in our actions*. That means we won't have *idols*—things that are more important to us than God.

God is spirit. He doesn't have a body like we do, so no one knows what he looks like. When idols were first made they were probably made to represent God and help people focus on him. But then people began worshiping the idol instead of God.

However, God is unlimited. He made everything. He is everywhere, knows everything, and can do anything. That means that whatever we use to represent God will be limited and too small. Then we begin to think that God is limited. As soon as we do that, we're trusting something with less power and ability to love us than God.

God made everything! No one

While Moses was receiving the Ten Commandments from God, the Israelites were already breaking the second commandment! They made and worshiped an idol.

thing he made can show us the whole truth about him.

Idol Temptations

"No problem!" we say. "I don't bow down to or worship my TV, skateboard, or computer. I don't worship my friends or family, either. That would be silly!" True, but they could still be idols to us—if we rely on them or things like them for what only God can give us. Only God can keep us safe, give us peace, make us wise, forgive our sins, take perfect care of us, and more. If we look to someone or something else for these things, we're putting our trust in something that isn't God. That's like worshiping idols.

For example, what would make you happy? Meeting your sports hero or favorite band?

A terrific best friend? A brand new, multispeed, top-of-the-line mountain bike? If you're unhappy and think these things will make you happy, they might be idols to you. But if you look to God and trust him for a happy life, he can provide you with all you need to be truly happy, including some of these things!

If God is first in our hearts, he'll be first in our actions. We'll turn to him for happiness, security, friends, and more. He'll be our priority in everything we do. And guess what! Not having idols makes a lot of sense. Looking for happiness in things that can't keep us happy gets disappointing. Going to a God who loves us is wonderful!

Idols Today

What do Buddhas, *go-shintai,* rivers, and elephant-headed statues have in common? They're all idols and/or sacred objects worshiped today. Buddhists bow down to statues of Buddha. *Go-shintai* are sacred objects in Japan's Shinto religion. The many Japanese gods or *kami* are said to live in them. To Hindus everything is sacred, so they might worship anything, including rivers. Hindus believe statues of "gods" like *Ganesha* (their elephant-headed god) actually are gods. Priests take care of the statues as they would people—feeding, washing, and dressing them.

The Bible says, "Dear children, keep away from statues of gods" (1 John 5:21).

Anything that becomes more important to us than God, or anything that we think will keep us happy, can be an idol.

Commandment Three:
Don't Misuse God's Name

Swearing with God's name breaks the third commandment.

What's in a Name?

We honor God in our hearts and with our actions. We also need to honor him with *our words*. That's what the third commandment is about: "*Do not misuse the name of the Lord your God*" (Exodus 20:7).

How are these names the same: Prince Charles, Superman, Billy Graham, Batman, Michael Jordan? When we hear them, whether the people are real or made-up, we know exactly whom we're talking about. If I said Billy Graham doesn't care about people or Superman is a weakling, you would think I didn't know what I was talking about. Names represent who we are to people. In fact, in many ways, our names are us. Misusing them misrepresents who we are. Say you love your friend Sandy, but when someone does something dumb, you say, "You pulled a Sandy!" What will people think Sandy is like? Dumb! You've misused Sandy's name. Instead, when we use someone's name, what we say about them should match who they are.

Truth Only

We can misuse God's name in two ways. First, we can say false things about him. Using God's name properly means matching what we say with what we believe and know is true. Imagine if your best friend, who knows you're honest, calls you a thief. She's misused your name by lying about you. That's like saying, "God doesn't hear me when I pray. He doesn't care." That's telling lies about God and saying he's different than he is. Instead, we should say, "God hears my prayers. He cares!"

Second, we can swear with God's name. When we use God's name like a swear word or when we're angry, it sounds like we're blaming God for our problems, saying he's cruel or unkind. If you said, "Dad!" whenever you got upset, would people think you loved your father and got along well with him? No!

When we misuse God's name, we deny how powerful and incredible he is and how much he loves us. That keeps us from trusting God and knowing who he really is. (Would you trust someone you believe doesn't care about you?) But God is love. He says, "Don't misuse my name," for our sakes. He knows that if we trust and respect his name, we'll come to love and know him more. We'll find out how wonderful he is and want him in our lives.

Swearing

What about swearing and bad language? It's wrong because: (1) People use swear words when they're angry and want to lash out and hurt someone. God doesn't want us to handle our emotions like that. He wants us to control ourselves and love people. (2) Swear words deal with crude, sinful subjects that are the opposite of what God wants for us. God wants us to respect and use the things he's given us the way they were designed to be used. Then we'll enjoy life more. (3) Swearing tells people about us. It shows them how we view things, how we handle our emotions, and what we believe. People who swear often show

they are crude, impolite, disrespectful, and not self-controlled.

"People will have to account for every careless word they have spoken" (Matthew 12:36). Swear words are careless words. Don't use them!

Moses was so angry at the Israelites for turning away from God that he smashed the stone tablets God had given him.

Commandment Four:

Keep the Sabbath

Jesus: The Sabbath

The first three commandments are about our relationship with God. The last six are about relationships with people. The fourth, *"Remember to keep the Sabbath day holy"* (Exodus 20:8), links the two kinds of commandments—like Jesus links us to God.

The fourth commandment tells us we need Jesus. We can't obey the last six commandments if we're not obeying the first three. God knew the only way we could do that was to have his laws on our hearts. And that would only happen when Jesus paid for our sins.

God made the world in six days and rested on the seventh (the Sabbath—"Sabbath" means rest). God didn't have to tell Adam and Eve to keep the Sabbath because they were already resting by trusting him! When they broke God's command-

God wants us to rest, relax, and trust him for everything.

ment, their rest ended. The seventh day represented Jesus. God knew from the beginning he'd have to send Jesus so we could rest from the hard work of looking after ourselves and trying to please him.

"Ever since God created the world, his work has been finished. The good news [of Jesus] was preached to us. Now we who have believed enjoy that rest. God rested from his work. Those who enjoy God's rest also rest from their work" (from Hebrews 4:1–3, 10). When we rest by trusting Jesus and God, we can obey the first three commandments, which helps us obey the others, too.

God said even farmland should have a Sabbath rest. So every seventh year Jewish farmers let the land rest and didn't sow crops on it.

Twice Reminded

So why take one day a week off if we're living every day in God's rest? It's like Christmas and Easter. We celebrate those special days as reminders that Jesus was born, died, and rose again. And one day a week we take a special day to remind ourselves how much God loves us, how well he takes care of us, and how Jesus made our relationship with God possible.

In fact, resting one day a week reminds us of two things. First, God cares for us and makes us right with him spiritually and mentally. Second, God cares about our physical needs. Look around. Everything works in cycles. Plants rest at night from making food, and during winter they rest to prepare for spring. We need rest, too. Imagine never sleeping or resting! You'd be staggering around, so exhausted you'd see triple! God gave us a rest day so we'd be refreshed for the next week.

Our faith and strength grow as we take one day to just rest and focus on what Jesus did for us.

The seven-day week has been around for a long time. The names we call the days of the week come from the Romans. Jews use different names.

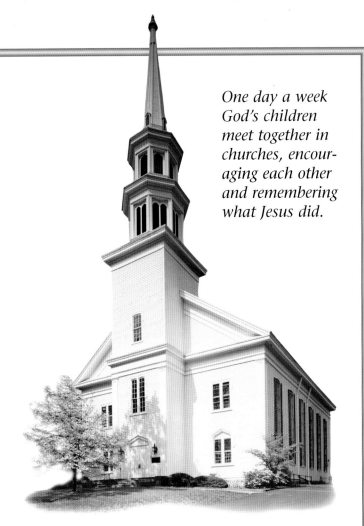

One day a week God's children meet together in churches, encouraging each other and remembering what Jesus did.

From Saturday to Sunday

In the Bible the Sabbath was celebrated on Saturday. These days we rest and meet with other Christians on Sunday. Why? Jesus rose from the dead on Sunday. He appeared to his disciples two Sundays in a row. And, seven weeks after Jesus rose, the Holy Spirit came on a Sunday. Also, the apostle John referred to Sunday as the "Lord's Day." "The Holy Spirit took complete control of me on the Lord's Day" (Revelation 1:10). In Acts, Christians met on Sunday. "On the first day of the week we met to break bread and eat together" (Acts 20:7). We follow their example and set aside Sunday to worship God and celebrate the rest he gives us.

WEDNESDAY   THURSDAY   FRIDAY   SATURDAY

YOM REVI'I   YOM CHAMISHI   YOM SHISHI   SHABBAT

Commandment Five:
Honor Your Parents

Listen to Mom

Now that our relationship with God is on track and Jesus makes it possible for us to obey God's commandments, the fifth commandment is about how that obedience is worked out with people. "If you don't love people, whom you've seen, how can you love God whom you haven't seen?" (from 1 John 4:20). This

commandment shows us that we learn to know God, get along with people, and obey the commandments by obeying our parents: "*Honor your father and mother*. Then you will live a long time in the land the Lord your God is giving you" (Exodus 20:12). The apostle Paul says, "Then things will go well with you" (Ephesians 6:3), applying this promise to all of our lives.

Did you hear about the baby zebra who decided her mom was silly to tell her to run away from lions? What about the kitten who pooh-poohed his mom's idea of avoiding angry dogs? Did these critters have long, happy lives? Nope! They ignored God's growth process of listening to their parents. God provided a perfect plan for how we grow and learn, too. Going against that plan is *not* a good idea. The plan calls for honoring and obeying parents who are honoring and obeying God.

Our parents and grandparents have been guiding and teaching us our whole lives. The skills they taught us when we were young have helped make us who we are today. When we honor our parents, we learn even more and our lives get even better.

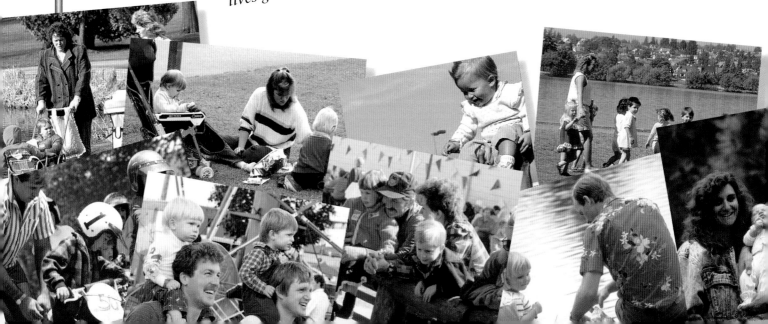

What Skills!

Here's how it works. If we honor our parents, we'll love and obey them, listen to their advice, treat them respectfully, and so on. Just look at the skills this requires: "Pleases" and "thank-yous," submission, kindness, no grumbling, polite voices, apologies, dropping something to do what we're told, and more. It takes your breath away!

These skills help things "go well" for us because they don't apply just to parents. They're useful everywhere, starting with God. Our parents are stand-ins for God. They teach us to obey God's rules. Obeying parents makes it easy to obey God. Bonus!

We need these skills with teachers, strangers, neighbors, bosses, and friends, too. If the skills are part of us because we constantly use them at home, we'll automatically use them with others. Will people be upset? No way! They'll be impressed. They'll trust us and enjoy being around us. And we'll be on our way to long, happy lives!

My Way

"Do I hafta?" Otherwise known as "I want my own way." Sound like Adam and Eve? We could go our own way without problems *IF* truth was *subjective* (changed with situations or when we decided) rather than *objective* (true no matter what). Would deciding gravity wasn't real make things fall *up?* Nope. Truth is as sure as gravity. Truth works according to God's character, which never changes. Truth is truth no matter what. It's that way because that's who God is, and because God wants us to have long, wonderful lives. We have those wonderful lives by living God's way and obeying our parents. That's the first step in God's growth process.

Honor "How-To's"

Honoring parents is: Cooperating when we're asked to do something; listening when our parents talk; doing our best; not talking back or using disrespectful tones of voice; respecting their "no" and not whining or trying to get the other parent to say "yes"; showing we trust them; letting them teach us; being obedient and kind; using respectful words.

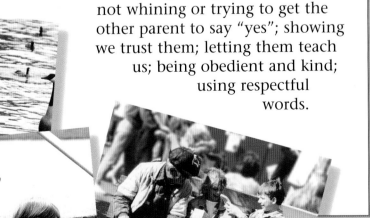

Commandment Six:
Don't Murder

Laser Mind

Okay, we've got the basics down: We love God and have a relationship with him through Jesus. We understand obedience and God's design for growth through honoring our parents. Now it's time to look at our relationships with other people. First, the foundation. The first commandment was about honoring God with our hearts. We start in the same place with people, honoring them *in our hearts*. The sixth commandment deals with this: *"Do not commit murder"* (Exodus 20:13).

Imagine a new tool installed in your mind that's controlled by thought. You think something—it happens. If you're reading and want to turn a page, a laser finger turns it. (Look, Mom, no hands!) Small laser beams steer your bicycle. Doors open with a thought. Burgers fry. Tired of a dirty room? Zzzzt. All gone. Frustrated with someone? *Zzzzt.* Singe their pants. Angry? ZZZZT! Sizzle the person.

STOP!

Thoughts are dangerous. With a tool like that, a thought could kill! Surprise! Jesus says it happens. He says being angry with someone is almost the same as murdering them (Matthew 5:21–22). In God's eyes, hating someone is murder! The thought equals the action. Better watch those thoughts!

Life Is a Gift

God invented life. He owns it and gave it to us as a beautiful gift. He's the only one with the right to say when to end it. Sometimes in the Bible God told people to fight wars or kill people—people who were sinning against him. The punishment for sin is death. But relax. God is kind, merciful, and loving. Jesus paid our penalty for sinning.

Respecting life by honoring and loving people in our hearts leads to great friendships.

Ways to Respect Life

OBEY GOD.
BE KIND.
HELP PEOPLE.
OBEY PARENTS.
BE FRIENDLY.
BE GENEROUS.
OBEY PEOPLE IN AUTHORITY.
ENCOURAGE PEOPLE.
SAY NICE THINGS.
KEEP YOUR TEMPER.
BE POLITE.

Jesus went to the heart of this commandment when he told us to love one another. He said the commandment doesn't just mean not murdering—it means loving and having positive attitudes in our hearts toward our neighbors. He said this to bless us with good relationships. He knows that when we love people we want only good for them. We don't think or say negative things about them. We don't judge them, or condemn them. The foundation for good relationships is love and respect.

God gives us this commandment because it's the best thing for us—it's the way life works. When we respect life and value it as precious, we treat people as God wants us to. Instead of "murdering" people in our thoughts, we love them and build positive, solid relationships. When we love our neighbors, friends, classmates, and families, we build them up and encourage them. Our relationships grow and we get the same back— great relationships and friendships. It's a wonderful payoff for respecting life and guarding our thoughts.

The Two Greatest Commandments

Jesus summed up the Ten Commandments in two. In fact, he summed up the whole Old Testament in two commandments: "'Love the Lord your God with all your heart and with all your soul. Love him with all your mind.' This is the first and most important commandment. And the second is like it. 'Love your neighbor as you love yourself'" (Matthew 22:37–39).

When we obey these commandments, we have the two greatest blessings—a wonderful, close relationship with God, and wonderful, close relationships with people.

Life couldn't get any better!

Love the Lord your God with all your heart and with all your soul. Love him with all your mind. Love your neighbor as yourself.

Commandment Seven:
Don't Commit Adultery

First People First

Now that the foundation of loving people from our hearts is in place, what relationships come first? In God's design it's the family. We should love everyone, but God has given us some relationships that are more important than others. The most important is our family; then relatives, close friends, other friends, and people in the community. In the family, the closest relationship is between husbands and wives (*spouses*). That includes physical closeness. The seventh commandment is about this: *"Do not commit adultery"* (Exodus 20:14).

Imagine that your best friend says, "Someone else is my best friend now." Or your dad says, "I've decided to make another kid my child instead of you." You'd feel lousy. Broken promises hurt. The worst broken promise ever is *adultery*—going outside the marriage and having a physical relationship with someone you're not married to, especially a person who's married to someone else.

Number-One Promise

When people marry, they promise to be faithful to each other and physically love *only each other* for the rest of their lives. This is the most important promise anyone can make to another person. Good relationships depend on trust. Where there's trust, people feel safe, loved, and content. This wonderful marriage relationship builds a strong foundation for other relationships. When parents are in love with each other, their families are content and secure. Solid families make happy, secure communities, which make peaceful countries. This is part of God's plan for us: A stable, wonderful world built out of happy marriages.

When husbands and wives keep their promises to each other, their families feel loved and secure.

Broken Hearts

When a husband or wife betrays this promise, it's like an earthquake destroying the marriage and family! Committing adultery doesn't work. It breaks hearts—and trust. It's very difficult to have close relationships with people we can't trust. When this key relationship breaks down, others follow. If someone breaks the most important promise by committing adultery, how can they be trusted to keep other promises? God knows life works this way. He gave us the seventh commandment so we'd have great relationships.

This commandment is related to the first three. In fact, marriage is like a picture of God and us. He's our number-one relationship. For us to go outside of that relationship to idols is like committing adultery on God. Ouch! Our relationship with God is the foundation for everything else in life. One thing for sure: God will never betray our trust!

Be committed. It's a great idea

Hollywood

Turn on the TV or a movie and what do you see? Someone breaking the seventh commandment. If it's not spouses cheating on each other, it's single people having physical relationships without being married. A physical relationship with *anyone* we're not married to breaks the seventh commandment. Even if we haven't met the person we'll marry, cheating on them at any time breaks the promise we'll make to them one day.

Hollywood teaches, "If you love someone, sleep with them." **Don't do it!** It doesn't work. God created life and relationships to work his way. Any other way breaks relationships and hurts us and the people we love. God's way is a blessing for us. Following God's way gives us a relationship where we know we're loved more than any other person in the world! Zowie!

21

Commandment Eight:
Don't Steal

To Lock or Not?

Okay, our relationships are based on love and trust. We're honoring and respecting people with our hearts. Remember how our heart for God shows in our actions? Our heart for people does, too. We need to honor and respect people *with our actions.* That's the eighth commandment: *"Do not steal"* (Exodus 20:15). It means we should value what others value.

Picture this: It's a sunny afternoon. You stop to play in the park and drop your backpack containing books, money, and a video game onto the grass. After playing, you rush home. Suddenly you realize you forgot your pack! No worries. It'll be there after supper. Sure enough, when you go back, it's there with everything in it. Is this possible? Or would you be afraid to let your pack out of your sight? Wouldn't it be great if your pack could be safe even over a weekend?

Any guesses why God gave us this eighth commandment? To help us build good relationships and safe communities. A community without theft would be fantastic! We wouldn't need house keys or locker locks—or any locks! People would trust each other, look out for each other, and value each other's property. That's what God wants for us.

Stealing is against the law wherever you go.

Greed or Generosity?

Unfortunately, few places are like that because the eighth commandment is broken a lot. So we lock our doors and use dead bolts, anti-theft devices, and alarm systems. We lock the windows at night and buy house insurance. Thieves don't respect other people's property. They don't value people—

We've done a comical movie set of what the Israelite camp around Mt. Sinai might have been like. How many businesses can you find?

how could anyone steal from someone they love?

Stealing shows that we think the key to life is things instead of trusting God and having great relationships with people. It shows that we think possessions will make us happy or keep us safe. Wrong! Our needs are not more important than other people's. Possessions are not more valuable than people. Stealing causes distrust and wrecks relationships. Who trusts a thief or wants one for a friend? When we steal, we aren't trusting God to look after us.

God loves us. He gives us everything we need, and then some. He even gives us extra to share with others. Giving instead of taking, helping instead of hurting, makes a wonderful community. When we're confident that God will give us what we need, and when we give to others, we have God's focus—people first.

More Than Possessions

Most of us have stolen something. Think about it. We can steal more than cars, clothes, money, or candy. Shoplifting is stealing. But so is cheating on a test—it's stealing someone's test score. Stealing is also: Refusing to share with others; not paying debts; breaking a promise; not doing our best when someone is paying us; slacking off or taking too many breaks when we're paid by the hour; keeping extra change. . . .

Ask, "Will this action love, respect, and value people?" If the answer is yes, you're keeping the commandment.

Commandment Nine:
Don't Lie

Little Is Big

As with God, we don't stop with respecting people in our hearts and with our actions. We also respect them *with our words*. The ninth commandment says: *"Do not give false witness against your neighbor"* (Exodus 20:16). At first this commandment meant testifying or being a witness at a trial. Jesus expanded it to mean all kinds of lies and relationships outside the courtroom.

A puny steering wheel tells a huge eighteen-wheeler truck where to go. A little rudder steers an ocean liner. A forest is burned by one careless match. Small can be powerful! When we're talking about the tongue, that's doubly true. The tongue is little,

but wow! the trouble it causes! With our tongue we can lie. Lying ruins reputations, gets innocent people in trouble, and destroys friendships.

Spaghetti Castle?

Remember how truth is truth no matter what? It's based on who God is. He is truth. He can never lie, so lying is always wrong. We can't go against God's character without having problems. That's just the way it works.

Think about what happens when we lie. Often we tell another lie to keep the first one from being discovered. That leads to another, and another. But without a doubt, it'll be found out. It's like trying to build a life-sized castle out of spaghetti. I don't think so! When the truth finally comes out, we get reputations as liars, people stop trusting us, and our relationships suffer.

We can also lie with our actions by making people think something is true when it isn't. Going into our room and closing the door so our parents think we're studying—when we're not—is lying. Will they trust us next time? No way!

We can lie by pretending to be someone we're not.

The ninth commandment was originally about lying in court. At that time most crimes that came to court had the death penalty. A lie killed someone!

Build 'Em Up

To Jesus, this commandment is about all of our words. The truth is, if we love people, we'll respect them by telling the truth to them and about them. We'll want to build them up and encourage them. We won't gossip or say nasty things. "Don't let any evil talk come out of your mouths. Say only what will help to build others up and meet their needs. Then what you say will help those who listen" (Ephesians 4:29). Positive, true words honor others.

How we tell the truth matters, too. "Speak the truth in love" (Ephesians 4:15). When we tell the truth, we should do it respectfully, valuing the person and building up the relationship. We should speak kindly out of love. If we can't say it lovingly, we shouldn't say it at all!

Our little tongues are powerful! We need to use them the way God wants us to—kindly, lovingly, truthfully—so that people are encouraged and want to get closer to God.

Positive Communication

Wanted: The lost art of encouraging, giving compliments, and gently being honest!

You can find it if you do these things: Tell people what you like about them; look for good things to say; if you hear people gossiping, change the subject or say something nice about the person instead; don't say, "You made me. . . ." No one can *make* you react; own your feelings—they belong to you. Even if someone is unkind, choose to react positively; listen first, speak later; speak respectfully; say kind things; say "please," "thank you," and "excuse me."

SCRAMBLED WORDS

Here are some words that show positive communication. Can you unscramble them?

TMCRNEGAENEUO.

SPMLEMOCNTI.

KYNHTSOAU-ILNSTE FTSIR.

SNELETPISO.

DIKN YOHSNTE.

25

Commandment Ten:
Don't Covet

Start Right

We're respecting God and people with our hearts, actions, and words. But the Pharisees kept God's commandments and Jesus told them, "You are like tombs painted white. . . . Beautiful on the outside . . . but full of the bones of the dead" (from Matthew 23:27). Actions aren't enough. The tenth commandment focuses our attention on our inner attitudes: *"Do not long for* [covet] *any-thing that belongs to your neighbor"* (Exodus 20:17).

How do you avoid turning a model airplane into something that looks like a barely recognizable, deformed tank—with pieces left over? You follow the directions, beginning with the very first piece. How do we keep from breaking God's commandments? We start with the first step—getting our thoughts and desires in line by not coveting.

Never Just One

The tenth commandment ties all the others together. God gave it to us to help us understand and keep the other commandments. It deals with the *reason* we break the commandments: Our inner thoughts and attitudes.

Coveting isn't just wanting what we don't have—we could go buy it. It's wanting what we have no right to have—someone else's stuff. When we covet, we put things before people and before God. We stop trusting God to take care of us, and life goes to pieces!

If you want an ice cream, go buy it. If you want his ice-cream, you're coveting!

Coveting can lead to breaking every other commandment. Look at King David in 2 Samuel 11. He coveted Uriah's wife (breaking the tenth commandment), committed adultery (the seventh), stole her from her husband (the eighth), deceived Uriah (the ninth), and even had Uriah killed (the sixth). God said David made fun of him by doing all this (the third). All these bad actions came from one wrong desire!

The Thought Counts

God cares about our actions and about where sin comes from—our inner selves. "Stealing, murder, adultery, greed, hate, cheating, wanting what belongs to others, and telling lies. All those evil things come from inside a person" (from Mark 7:21–22). To obey God's commandments, we need to change the way we think— not only what we feel, do, or say. When we think that something should be ours and want it badly, it becomes a "god" and idol to us. We break the first two commandments— and the trouble really begins!

God loves us. He gave us this commandment to protect us from the consequences of breaking the others. (Read 2 Samuel 13–18 to find out the awful consequences of David's sins.)

Garbage In, Garbage Out

What we "feed" ourselves—what we read, watch, and let ourselves think—eventually comes out of us. Bad TV shows affect our hearts and minds. Watching violence makes us think violence is the answer to problems. Watching ads telling us what we *have* to have starts us thinking that those things will make us happy. Then we covet them.

God wants us to learn how he views things, and then choose to think his way. He'll work in us, changing our hearts and desires, and putting new hearts in us. "Let your way of thinking be completely changed. Then you will be able to test what God wants for you. And you will agree that what he wants is right. His plan is good and pleasing and perfect" (Romans 12:2).

People often think things or money will make them happy. That can lead to breaking God's commandments.

The Heart of It

God molds us into the people he wants us to be, like a potter molds his clay.

By Heart

Now we have all we need to obey God's commandments all the time. Not! One thing is probably clear: It's not that simple. We can't completely obey God's commandments on our own.

Do you need help to tie your shoelaces or count to a hundred? Would you forget your name or how to ride a bike? No. You know these things by heart. Once you've learned them, they stay learned. They're in your heart and mind forever. Wouldn't it be great to have God's commandments in our hearts and minds like that?

It can happen! In the beginning, God's laws were in Adam and Eve's hearts. He can put them in ours, too. In fact, he said he would: "I will put my law in their minds. I will write it on their hearts. I will be their God. And they will be my people" (Jeremiah 31:33).

Jesus makes this possible. He draws us into God's Sabbath rest and bridges the gap between God and us. He died on the cross and paid for our sins. When we accept what Jesus did and ask God to forgive us, he does. He comes to live in us and change our hearts so his commandments can be in our hearts, just as he's always wanted.

Carved by Love

It all comes back to love. Love carves the commandments on our hearts. God gave them to us because he loves us and wants the best for us. The commandments are all about love—for God and people. And obeying them leads to more love.

Will God just tell us what he wants and walk away? Does a potter throw a lump of clay on his wheel and say, "Be a pot"? He'd wait a lo-o-ong time. No. He works on the clay, takes out bad parts, and carefully and lovingly molds it into the shape he wants. Then he bakes it so it will last for years.

Making us into who God wants is way more work and God does it far more lovingly than any potter. He trains, molds, and makes us into people we'll love to be. It's all part of his growth process. Our job is to put ourselves into his loving hands and choose to obey him. We let God work in us, building his commandments and love deeper and deeper into us until they're written on our hearts—carved by love. "May [God] make you holy through and through. May your whole spirit, soul and body be kept free from blame. . . . The One who has chosen you is faithful. He will do all these things" (1 Thessalonians 5:23–24).

Growing the Relationship

Through Jesus we know God personally. We'll want our relationship with him to grow! Here's how. (1) Talk to him. God gave us prayer so we could tell him about our lives, ask him things, and get answers. (2) Read his book. The Bible explains how God designed everything to work. It tells us who God is and helps us understand what he wants from us. (3) Hang out with his friends. God's people meet together at church, learn from each other, and encourage and help each other grow as his children.

Getting to know God is like building any friendship—it takes time and togetherness.

Unravel the strings to match the situation with the commandment that is being broken.

- Billy comes home from school and says he hates his teacher.
- Martha's mom tells her to clean her room, but she watches TV instead.
- Victor's dad left his wife for another woman.
- Blair's room is a shrine to Michael Jordan.
- Natalie spends all her spare time polishing her new bike.
- Joseph tells his friends that God doesn't answer prayer.
- Donna says she took only two cookies, but she really took four.
- Al's brother works seven days a week at the gas station.
- Julia is angry because she is the only kid on her block without a pool.
- Mike finds a wallet in the street and takes it home and hides it.

1. Do not worship any other gods besides me. Ex. 20:3
2. Do not make idols or bow down to idols. Ex. 20:4
3. Do not misuse my name. Ex. 20:7
4. Remember to observe the Sabbath; keep it holy. Ex. 20:8
5. Honor your father and mother. Ex. 20:12
6. Do not murder. Ex. 20:13
7. Do not commit adultery. Ex. 20:14
8. Do not steal. Ex. 20:15
9. Do not lie. Ex. 20:16
10. Do not covet your neighbor's belongings. Ex. 20:17

29

Is It Wrong?

Q **What if one parent says you can watch a certain movie, and then the other one says you can't?**

A If one parent tells you no, accept that and don't go looking for permission from your other parent. Some kids go back and forth between parents until the one who said no gives in and says okay. That's wrong because it dishonors the parent who said no. If Mom or Dad says you can't do something (like watch a certain movie), nicely ask why. That will help you understand the reason for the no. But don't argue, complain, or whine about it. Instead, say thank you and obey.

God wants us to honor and obey our parents. That's how God keeps kids safe and gives them what they need to grow up. Obeying and honoring your parents will help you learn the things you need to live a happy and productive life.

Q **Why is it wrong to do something if all the other kids do it?**

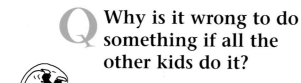

A If something is wrong, it's wrong, no matter how many people do it. Suppose a group of your friends started throwing stones through windows in the neighborhood. Would it be okay just because everyone did it? Of course not! It would be wrong whether *one* person or *everyone in school* did it.

If a lot of kids swear, cheat, lie, do drugs, drink, smoke, disobey their parents, shoplift, or do something else that's wrong, don't think you have to do it, too. If the group you hang around with does wrong things and pressures you to join them, find another group. You should do what's right, even if you're the only one. That's what God wants.

Q **Is it okay for Mom and Dad to lie to you about your Christmas presents?**

A God wants us always to be truthful. But that doesn't mean we have to answer every question, nor does it mean that we have to tell everything we know. If you ask your parents, "What did you get me for Christmas?" or "Did you get me a bike for Christmas?" they can say something like: "I'm not going to tell you because I want you to be surprised."

Be careful not to make excuses for lying. Don't lie and then make up a reason for doing it. When it comes to giving gifts, there are ways to surprise people and make them feel special without lying to them.

Q **Is it all right to say bad things if there's no one to hear?**

A If something is wrong, it's always wrong. So swearing, lying, and saying bad things about others are wrong, even if no one hears. God knows what's going on; he sees and hears everything.

That's why a true test of your character comes whenever you think no one is watching or listening. If you really believe swearing is wrong, you won't do it, period. You won't look for opportunities to do it when no one is around to catch you. Work hard at speaking and *thinking* what is good and right, even when no one is around, because that's what really matters. Even what you think counts; God knows our every thought.

And if anyone does find out what you said in private, they'll know that you can be trusted. Live every moment as a service to God.

JASON'S IMAGINATION

Adapted from *103 Questions Children Ask About Right From Wrong*, Tyndale House Publishers, 1995. Used by permission

Strong Foundation

Build Wisely

Imagine a construction company building a house right on top of the grass. When it was done, a big wind or enough (very strong) people might be able to slide that house anywhere they wanted—a new type of mobile home! Every solid house needs a foundation dug deep into the ground so it will stand firm even in the strongest wind. That house will be even stronger when the foundation is set into bedrock.

We need to build our lives on a solid foundation—the Ten Commandments. The foundation of the Ten Commandments is set into the solid bedrock of God's love. In the commandments God gave us everything we need for wonderful, solid lives. The Ten Commandments cover all of life. They're the keys to happiness.

Bedrock Love

Everything about God has to do with love. He gave us his commandments out of love for us. He wants to be our Father—to look after, care for, protect, teach, and guide us.

Through his commandments, he shows us how we can have the best lives possible.

The commandments don't only come out of love, they're all about love. We love God through the first four and people through the last six. We treat God and people with love, respect, and honor, with our hearts, actions, words, and thoughts. If we love God, obeying the first commandments will come naturally. And if we love people, so will obeying the last ones.

The result? More love! We experience God's love for us. And people love us. We get to know God and people, and we grow close to them. All our relationships are built on this solid foundation of love and respect. That leads to the wonderful lives God planned for us! What could be better?